Visit me at www.GardeningWithJason.com ... ...s and advice
or follow me at www.YouTube.com/Ownin, ...ent for my video
diary and tips. Join me on Facebook at
www.Facebook.com/OwningAnAllotment.

Follow me on Instagram and Twitter as @allotmentowner for regular
updates, tips and to ask your gardening questions.

If you have enjoyed this book, please leave a review on Amazon. I read
each review personally and the feedback helps me to continually
improve my books and provide you with more helpful books to read.

Once you have read this book, you will be offered a chance to download
one of my books for free. Please turn to the back of the book to find out
how to get your free book.

TABLE OF CONTENTS

INTRODUCTION

Lavender is probably one of the most popular herbs that people grow. It has a delightful fragrance, some culinary uses, attracts bees and looks great in any garden particularly when it flowers.

While it is relatively easy to grow, it has its own set of foibles that can make it a tricky plant to keep alive, but is well worth persevering with. Whether you grow a few plants in pots or borders or make a lavender hedge, this plant is surprisingly useful.

This book will provide you with everything you need to know about lavender, from growing this gorgeous plant to caring for it and harvesting the flowers and leaves. You will find out how to use the plant in the home and kitchen, as well as its beauty and health uses. This is not only a good looking, hardy plant, but one that is versatile and benefits every garden.

As you read this book, you will find out all about lavender, from its origins and use with humans to the folklore that has become associated with this plant.

Lavender is not that difficult to grow, providing you give it the right growing conditions. The biggest mistake people make with lavender, and you see this in potted plants in particular, is that the soil mix is not right, so the plant struggles and eventually dies. However, given the right conditions, lavender will thrive with minimal care and live for a good number of years.

One of the best things about lavender, in my opinion, is that it is a low maintenance plant. It does not need a lot of attention, is barely bothered by pests and diseases when grown at home and needs a quick prune once a year to maintain its shape. You can't ask for better than that in a good looking plant!

There are literally hundreds of lavender varieties on the market, though you will only see a few varieties in the stores. Most of the more unusual varieties are best bought from specialist nurseries. However, for most uses, the more common varieties like Hidcote are the best varieties anyway. Many of the other varieties are better as ornamental plants rather than for culinary or beauty uses.

Lavender is less popular now than it was thirty or forty years ago as a perfume, but it is still popular as a scent in air fresheners. Today the scent of lavender on a person is commonly associated with grandmothers, showing it was much more popular in yesteryear. Despite this, lavender is still used in many beauty products today because of its scent and its many healing and health benefits. It is very good for your skin and is naturally antiseptic.

In the kitchen, lavender has some surprising uses. While in the past it was commonly used, it fell out of favour, probably because it was very easy to overwhelm a dish. In recent years it has seen a resurgence of interest as chefs look for new and different ingredients. However, there is one thing to be aware of when you are using lavender for cooking that you will find out later in this book.

Lavender oil is probably something most of us are familiar with. The essential oil has many uses and is a fantastic ingredient in home-made beauty products. It is commonly used in the home from scenting pot-pourri to being used to relax and calm.

Growing lavender is a very rewarding experience. It is a beautiful plant that grows well, smells fantastic and is wonderful for our native wildlife. Enjoy reading this book and finding out how you can grow this plant at home plus how you can use it around your home! It is one plant that will earn its keep.

One of the most popular vegetables to grow at home is the courgette or zucchini plant. The fruits are relatively expensive to buy in the stores, particularly out of season, yet the seeds are cheap and the plant extremely easy to grow. A single plant can produce twenty or thirty fruits in a season, and most people grow several plants.

History, Origins and Folklore

The name lavender, or Lavandula, derives from the Latin word 'lavare' meaning to wash. The Romans used lavender in bath water not only for its scent, but also for its many therapeutic properties, including its natural antiseptic properties.

In the book, 'A New Herball' written by the famous naturalist William Turner in the mid-16th century, he explained how the name derived from the Latin,

"Because wyse men founde by experience that it was good to washe mennes heades with, which had any deceses therein, or wieknes that come of a colde cause…"

This seems to imply that lavender was used to treat mental disorders and possibly stress. One of the main properties of lavender is that it helps you to relax and eases stress. It also demonstrates lavenders healing abilities as it is not only antiseptic, but also has anti-inflammatory and antifungal properties.

In Greece, lavender was called 'Nardus' after the Syrian city of Naarda where lavender was commonly sold. Some referred to this plant as 'nard' and in the Bible, Mary Magdalene opened an alabaster box of spikenard and used the oil to anoint Jesus's feet. Biblical researchers believe this spikenard to be lavender, though a much earlier variety. Spikenard and nard have been used to refer to a number of different plants and later on, these words became strongly associated with ginger.

In 1922 when Howard Carter broke into the Egyptian Pharaoh Tutankhamen's tomb, he discovered lavender that had been buried with this ancient king over 3000 years previously. After all this time, it still retained some of its aroma. To find this herb in a tomb of such an important person shows how highly the Ancient Egyptians regarding lavender.

Lavender was considered a valuable plant in the past. During Pliny's era in Rome (23-79 AD), nardus blossoms were sold for 100 Roman denarii per pound. For the same money, a Roman could have bought ten liters of a cheap wine or ten pounds of bread, so you can see how valuable this herb was considered.

The Romans referred to lavender as 'Asarum'. The name derives from the belief that the poisonous asp viper lived in lavender plants and so this plant should be approached cautiously.

The use of lavender migrated with the Roman army and soon it spread throughout the Roman Empire where it became naturalized and popular with the local inhabitants across Europe. In northern England in the 12th Century, washerwomen were referred to as 'Lavenders' because they used this herb to scent freshly washed linen. They believed that lavender kept moths and insects away from the linen. It is from this practice that the term 'to be laid up in lavender' originates. In books from this time, lavender has been referred to by a variety of names including 'Llafant' and 'Lavyndull'.

Since the 16th century, England has cultivated lavender and grown it as a commercial crop. The counties of Norfolk and Surrey were deemed particularly suitable for growing this herb. In texts from the 1800s, English lavender oil is obviously prized as it sold for a much higher price than French or other European lavender. English lavender was valued as its fragrance was, by far, the best of all varieties.

Queen Elizabeth I of England (1533 – 1603) loved lavender and encouraged it to be grown. She was particularly fond of lavender flower conserve and lavender buds baked in cookies. The wife of Charles I, Queen Henrietta Maria (1609-1669) preferred the white cultivar not for its fragrance, but for its look. By the mid-1700s, lavender was popular as an edging on stately home and royal gardens.

In Ireland during the 17th century, lavender became popular as a lawn, kept just a few inches tall with a scythe. The gardens of Moira Castle in County Down supposedly had a lavender lawn over an acre in size in 1683, but today that garden is lost and the castle stands as a ruin.

In 1857, the book 'The Art of Perfumery' claimed the best lavender was grown in a town called Mitcham in Surrey, England and that all other varieties were inferior. This superior oil was used in lavender water while the inferior versions were used to perfume soaps.

Lavender was popular outside of the UK and before World War I, a 'lavender still' would travel around towns and villages in Europe, distilling lavender into an essential oil. In Northern Africa, lavender was valued and used for washing and perfuming bodies.

This herb has a long history of association with humans and, as such, as garnered a great deal of folklore. For example, in Tuscany, Italy, Lavender was considered to counteract the evil eye.

Lavender had some association with the plague as a component of something called 'Marseilles Vinegar' or 'Four Thieves Vinegar', invented by Richard Forthave. This concoction supposedly protected people from the plague. Although there were some variations in the recipe regionally, lavender was a common ingredient between them all, probably to mask the smell of other ingredients which often included garlic and vinegar.

This history behind Four Thieves Vinegar is a little muddled and two main versions of this story survive. In the first, the thieves were captured before a plague outbreak and invented the vinegar to protect themselves when they were sentenced to bury plague victims. In the second, they invented the mixture to allow them to safely burgle plague victim's houses and traded the recipe in return for lenience when they were captured.

In both Spain and Portugal, lavender was burned on bonfires during St. John's Day, which helped to ward off evil. On St. Luke's Day in the 15th and 16th centuries, young maidens sipped a lavender tea that they hoped would give them a dream of their true love. Young men put sprigs of lavender under their pillows to encourage them to ask a lady to marry them. Wives also used lavender to ensure their husband's marital passion! Prostitutes wore lavender to attract customers as well as to protect themselves from violence and cruelty.

Yet, according to folklore, combine lavender with rosemary and instead of encouraging love, it preserves virtue!

There are many traditional medicinal uses of lavender, many of which have never been researched by modern scientists. Whether these work or not are the subject of a great deal of debate, but they are interesting purely from a historical point of view.

Lavender was used as an insect repellent by soaking chunks of cotton in lavender oil and hanging it around the next. This supposedly warded off bugs and insects, though some sources specific it protected against worms.

Mix lavender with turpentine or spirit of wine and you are left with Oleum spicoe, which was used to cure stiff joints or sprains. Lavender oil was also used to stimulate paralyzed limbs.

Lavender oil was taken orally, but nowadays this is not recommended. It was used to treat a wide variety of complaints including hysteria and palsy while acting as a strong stimulant. Mixing lavender and rosemary oil in wine for a week with crushed nutmeg, red sandalwood and cinnamon bark produced a cordial known as "Palsy Drops" which was a very popular medicinal product.

Many people rub lavender oil into their temples as it helps with nervous headaches and lavender tea helps headaches from tiredness. Inhabitants of the Mediterranean regions used to wear lavender in their hats as it prevented sun headaches.

Too much lavender is bad for you, which is one reason why it is no longer recommended orally. It can cause griping and colic, but in extreme doses it causes narcotic poisoning and death by convulsions!

Lavender is also considered an antiseptic herb, and it would often be burnt in rooms where people were sick.

As you can see, lavender has a long history of use by humans and has been used to treat a wide variety of complaints. Modern herbalists and perfumists love lavender. It is still a very popular scent and for many people is an 'olde worlde' scent, reminding them of grandparents or the past. Today it is most commonly used as a perfume or the essential oil is used for relaxation, but it has many other uses, which you will learn as you read this book.

HOW TO GROW LAVENDER

Lavender is a great plant to grow at home, being equally happy in containers or in the ground. It will thrive in almost any soil, though prefers poor to moderately fertile soils that are free-draining. It grows well in alkaline or chalky soils, though is much happier in full sun.

It will grow in heavy soils like clay, though its lifespan is reduced as it becomes woodier at the base. Digging in organic matter and gravel improves drainage and helps the lavender live longer. Planting on a mound also helps with drainage and if you are planting a hedge, build up a ridge of soil to put the plants in to keep their roots out of wet soil.

Once established, lavender is generally drought tolerant and is suitable for planting in gravel gardens or on coast.

Most lavender cultivars need 3 feet/90cm between plants, though if you are making a lavender hedge, reduce this spacing. Smaller cultivars need to be 12"/30cm apart and larger cultivars need a little bit more room, 18"/45cm.

Some lavender cultivars are fully hardy, whereas others are half-hardy and tender. Check the specific cultivars before buying and make sure you get one that is as hardy as you need it. In cooler areas, people grow tender and half-hardy cultivars in containers so they can be moved indoors and protected from frost in winter.

Generally, lavender is planted in the spring, though hardy varieties can be planted as late as September or October.

Make sure that you have prepared the soil appropriately before planting lavender. It will last longer and provide a better display of flowers if it has the ideal growing conditions. It is a generally tolerant plant though and will grow in most conditions, but it really objects to overly wet soils.

Growing from Seed

It is possible to grow lavender from seed, though a lot of people prefer to buy pre-grown plants purely because of the time it takes for seed grown lavender to mature. Seeds can be collected from dry seed heads, though be aware that they will not breed true and you could end up with different colored flowers. If you want to grow a specific cultivar, then growing from cuttings is the best way to get new plants. Lavender Lady and Munstead are two varieties that grow well from seed.

Start the seeds early spring, ideally germinating them in a seed tray placed on a heat mat or in a warm spot. A temperature of 65-70F/18-21C is required for successful germination.

Use a light soil that drains well, so mix in plenty of vermiculite otherwise the seeds get soggy and rot. It takes anything up to three months for the seeds to germinate and longer for them to look like lavender. Keep them well watered but do not allow them to remain damp. Position them in full sun for best growth.

Once there are several sets of leaves on your new seedlings, you can plant them out into their final location. However, check them regularly as they will get dislodged and knocked over very easily. When they are settled in place, they will grow quite slowly during their first year, but by the second year they will be good sized plants.

Growing from seed is a cheap way to get plenty of lavender plants, but as the seeds are slow to germinate and you are unlikely to see flowers in the first year, most people do not use this method. However, if you are after a large number of plants, then this is by far the cheapest way to get lots of plants so long as you are patient.

Growing from Store Bought Plants

Most people buy plants from stores that are already a couple of years old. The older and larger the plant, the more expensive they usually are. If you are patient, then you can buy plug plants quite cheaply, which are small, one-year-old plants. These are available online from gardening stores and are a great way to get lots of plants cheaply.

Store bought plants can either be kept in the containers they come in, transferred to larger containers or planted out in the ground, providing they are a hardy cultivar. Plant them as per the instructions above and ensure they are not in a damp location.

Growing from Cuttings

To grow more plants that are true to the cultivar, propagate lavender by cuttings. Softwood or semi-ripe cutting, taken in early summer, or hardwood cuttings from new growth, taken in late fall after flowering, are the easiest way to get more plants of the same variety.

Taking cuttings in the summer is by far the easiest and more reliable method of propagating these plants. Taking cuttings is not difficult and does not need any specialist equipment. All you need is:

- Sharp knife/scissors
- 4"/10cm pots
- Multipurpose compost
- Rooting hormone (powder or liquid)
- Clear polythene bags
- Elastic bands

Look for side shoots that you can take as cuttings. Pull each one carefully away from the stem, leaving a heel or thin strip of bark attached to it. This is important as this is where the roots of the new plant are doing to develop. Trim excess bark off the heel using a sharp knife.

Remove any lower leaves so there is a length of bare stem that can be pushed down into the soil. Dip this stripped end into rooting hormone and then push the stem down into the soil. Plant four or five cuttings around the edge of each 4"/10cm plot.

Water the compost well, then put a clear plastic bag over the pot, sealing it in place with an elastic band. This creates a humid, greenhouse effect that helps the cuttings retain moisture while they root.

Leave the pots in a warm, but shady spot and they will root in four to six weeks. Once they have rooted, cut the corner off the bag to provide some ventilation. A few weeks later, remove the bag completely.

Allow the cuttings to establish a proper root system, then transfer them to individual pots.

Growing in Containers

Lavender grows well in containers, though prefers larger containers to achieve full size (12-16"/30-40cm). Smaller plants can be grown in smaller pots, but they will need potting on as the plant matures.

Use a good quality compost and mix in about a third of coarse grit to improve the drainage. Lavender will also appreciate some slow release fertilizer granules mixing in with the compost.

Water the container regularly during the summer months, but in winter, reduce the watering and keep the plant a little on the dry side. This prevents it from becoming waterlogged and the roots rotting. Either move the plant into a cold greenhouse or position it in the rain shadow of a wall.

Tender or half-hardy cultivars are best in containers so they can be moved to a sheltered spot or indoors in winter. Varieties such as Lavendula canariensis, Lavendula pinnata and Lavendula lanata do not tolerate the cold and so are best planted in containers.

Virtually all Lavandula stoechas (French lavender) cultivars and Lavandula pedunculata subsp. Pedunculata are suitable for containers as they are not hardy. Most hybrid lavender plants are also not fully hardy and so are best growing in containers so they can be moved inside.

The best type of containers for lavender are large, terracotta pots with good drainage holes. Although you can use plastic pots, they tend to retain a bit too much moisture which the lavender plants do not like.

Caring for Lavender Plants

Prune lavender every year to maintain a compact habit and a good shape. Once the plant is established, use secateurs or sharp scissors to cut off the flower stalks and one inch of this year's growth, ensuring some green growth remains. This is usually done in late summer, though some people recommend pruning in spring. From my experience, it is better to do it in late summer once it has finished flowering because the plant can continue to grow if the winter is mild.

Left to its own devices, lavender becomes leggy, woody and the number of flowers diminish. Unfortunately, once a lavender plant becomes woody, it produces very little new growth. Pruning lavender every year extends its lifetime, otherwise it is very short lived.

Woody lavender plants can sometimes be brought back to life. In mid-August, prune the plant back to just above a green shoot. New shoots should appear within the next four to six weeks. If no new shoots appear, then the plant is best replaced. Remember that you have to leave some green growth when pruning for the plant to recover. If you cut out all evidence of green shoots, then you the plant is finished off as it does not grow back from the woody growth.

Protect tender and half hardy varieties from the cold. Some frost hardy varieties will survive outdoors in a sheltered spot through a mild winter, but a cold winter will kill them. These tender varieties should not be pruned any later than September to give them time to recover before winter sets in. Hardy varieties can be left in the garden all year or planted in the ground. These are typically hardy down to about 5F/-15C.

Unusual tender varieties, such as Lavandula denata, can be deadheaded and pruned only when the plant becomes untidy.

Pruning is essential for lavender plants. Pruned properly and regularly, most lavender plants will live for between 15 and 20 years if they growing in the right soil conditions.

Lavender benefits from a sprinkling of potash on the soil, which encourages the plant to produce more flowers with a better color. Avoid high nitrogen feeds of manure as this encourages the plant to produce excessive amounts of leaves and it ends up all green growth and no flowers, flopping over because of the amount of foliage.

Putting an inch of good quality compost around the base of your lavender plants in spring will provide them with all the nutrients they need throughout the growing season. Remember that lavender likes a nutrient poor soil and overfeeding it will cause damage to the plant.

Also remember that lavender plants like to be dry. The common mistake gardeners make with lavender is to overwater it. It is sensitive to excessive watering, so ensure it has dried out thoroughly before watering it any more.

Lavender Pests and Diseases

For such a popular plant, lavender suffers from very few diseases and pests. It generally will grow quite happily and not have any problems. Although it can get a couple of diseases, they are very rare and you are unlikely to ever encounter them unless you are growing on a large scale or close to a commercial grower. The biggest problem you will have with lavender is that the roots get too wet!

However, there is the potential of problems, so here are the pests and diseases that could affect your lavender plants:

- **Alfa Mosaic Virus** – a very easy disease to spot as the leaves turn yellow and contort as they curl up. The virus is spread by insects and from your hands. If you see any infected plants, remove them immediately, avoiding using your hands to touch the plant. Burn the infected material or dispose of it in the trash.
- **Lavender Shab Disease (Phomopsis lavandula)** – a fungal infection that attacks and kills the stems of the plant. The most obvious symptom of this disease is when the shoots suddenly wilt, even though the plant has been getting plenty of water. If you use a magnifying glass to inspect an infected plant, you will see tiny black shapes known as pycnidia coming out of the bark. These contain the spores which are then spread on the wind. This is a very rare disease, but if you do encounter it, remove and burn infected plants immediately.
- **Wet Feet** – although not a disease, this is probably the biggest killer of lavender plants. When buying a new plant, check the soil around the roots is not too wet, particularly when buying plants in winter. With wet feet, the roots die and the stem is easily removed from the roots.
- **Cuckoo Spit** – This is not much of a threat to the plant, more of an unattractive irritation. This is where clumps of what looks like spit forms on the plant, usually on the joint between a branch and a stem. Inside this is a capsid bug that will feed on your plant's sap. In small quantities they do not do any harm, but if a plant is

seriously infested then it can damage a plant, particularly if it is already weak or struggling. These are easy to get rid of, just spray water on them and they will come off.

- **Whitefly** – Sometimes you can find whitefly on lavender plants, but it is rare for the infestation to be fatal. If the whitefly population is left unchecked, then the plant may not grow as much and the leaves can yellow. Spraying with water will remove adult whiteflies and the younger ones can be caught on special traps. The main problem with whitefly is that it can move on to other plants, particularly vegetable plants, where they are more damaging.
- **Aphids** – Although they may land on lavender plants, they rarely cause damage like they do on other plants. However, be aware that aphids can transmit the deadly Alfa Mosaic Virus so should be treated as soon as they are seen.

LAVENDER VARIETIES

There are currently more than 45 different species of lavender with over 450 different varieties. There are still more varieties that are yet to be classified.

Lavender belongs to the genus Lavandula. The two most common species in Northern latitudes are Lavandula angustifolia and Lavandula x intermedia, also known as lavandin which is a cross between L. latifolia and L. angustifolia. In general, the lavandin plants have longer stems than L. angustifolia and flower later in the year.

Choosing a variety can be quite tricky because there are so many out there. If you are buying from a store, then you will usually only find one or possible two varieties. Most of these varieties need to be ordered from specialist suppliers, but some can be found in your local garden center. If you are unsure of what variety to grow, then Hidcote or Munstead, both of which are readily available are a good choice. These can be used for health, beauty and culinary purposes and are generally hardy plants.

When deciding the variety to grow, think about what you are growing lavender for? This will help you decide which cultivar is best for your garden.

- Landscaping – when growing lavender for landscaping you need to consider the size of the plant when it is mature and the space you have available. As lavender can produce flowers that are pink, white and every shade of purple, you need to determine what color flower will fit with your garden color scheme. Another consideration is hardiness as you are likely to be planting in the ground. You can use tender varieties in cooler areas if you are willing to treat the plants as annuals and replace them every year, though in warmer or sheltered areas, tender cultivars grow well outside.
- Dried Buds – the buds of most varieties can be saved for crafting purposes, but some cultivars have a stronger flavor and a dark color that are more suitable for health or culinary use. There are also some varieties that are much easier to remove the individual buds from.
- Culinary Buds – lavender has a number of uses in the kitchen and is surprisingly nice in a wide variety of dishes. Generally, if you taste a flower bud and it tastes okay, then it is good to use in cooking.
- Crafting – the craft you are thinking about may determine the lavender cultivar you grow. Do you want long or short stems? Pale or dark flowers?
- Fresh Cut – if you are cutting lavender then you may want to grow a number of cultivars that flower throughout the season so you have fresh flowers for a longer period of time.
- Essential Oil – different cultivars produce different amounts of oil and the scent can vary between varieties. The oil is also affected by the summer heat, the rain in spring and the altitude you are growing at! Aromatherapy practitioners will only use L. angustifolia essential oil, not lavandins.

French Lavender

The following list is some of the best lavender varieties for these uses. This is not a definitive list and you can certainly use the lavender varieties for things other than those specified here. Typically, you will only find a few of these varieties in the stores. Many of these cultivars will only be available from specialised nurseries and suppliers.

- Lavandula angustifolia (English Lavender) – the hardiest of the lavenders being hardy down to 14F/-10C to 5F-15C and will survive all but the coldest of winters.

The following varieties make for excellent hedging plants and are English lavenders that produce purple/blue flowers.

- L. angustifolia 'Ashdown Forest' – produces pale flowers from early summer on grey/green foliage. Grows to 20"/50cm high and 30"/75cm wide.
- L. angustifolia 'Hidcote' – a commonly found cultivar that has dense, dark-violet colored flowers on stems of up to 9"/23cm long from late June, onwards. The foliage is grey/green in color and compact and bushy. This cultivar grows to 24"/60cm high and 30"/75cm wide.
- L. angustifolia 'Munstead' – a popular cultivar with compact, mid-green foliage and very lavender blue flowers. Grows up to 18"/45cm high and 24"/60cm wide.
- L. angustifolia 'Lodden Blue' – grey/green foliage and lots of violet blue flowers on spikes up to 7"/18cm long appearing from early July. Grows to 18"/45cm high and 28"/70cm wide.
- L. angustifolia 'Royal Purple' – grey/green foliage with long, dark purple flowers from early June. Grows up to 30"/75cm high and 36"/90cm wide.

These are some popular dwarf cultivars that are ideal for the front of flower borders or for a lower hedge:

- L. angustifolia 'Little Lottie' (Clarmo)– compact, grey/green foliage with pale pink flowers appearing from late June. Grows up to 15"/40cm high and 26"/65cm wide.
- L. angustifolia 'Miss Muffet' (Schlomis) – grey/green foliage with violet/purple flowers from late June. Grows up to 12"/30cm tall and 20"/50cm wide.
- L. angustifolia 'Nana Alba' – light green leaves and lots of white flowers from late June. Grows to 12"/30cm high and wide.

These cultivars all have variegated foliage so make for an unusual addition to the herb garden.

- L. angustifolia 'Garden Beauty' (Lowmar) – yellow variegated leaves appear in spring, fading to a cream color in summer and then turning green in winter. This compact plant produces lovely lavender/purple flowers from mid-June. Grows up to 20"/50cm high and 28"/70cm wide.
- L. x intermedia 'Walburton's Silver Edge' (Walvera) – a hybrid with grey/green leaves with cream edges. It produces lavender/violet flowers from late July. Grows up to 30"/75cm high and 36"/90cm wide.

These varieties have silver foliage and, again, look quite unusual when grown in the garden:

- L. x chytoriae 'Richard Gray' – silvery grey leaves and beautiful purple flowers appearing in early July. Grows up to 20"/50cm tall and 32"/80cm wide.
- L. x chyoriae 'Sawyers' – silvery grey leaves with tall, bushy lilac/blue flowers from early July. Grows to about 28"/70cm tall and 48"/120cm wide.

These varieties have pink flowers:

- L. angustifolia 'Hidcote Pink' – grey/green leaves and pale pink/lavender flowers appearing from late June. Grows to about 20"/50cm tall and 28"/70cm wide.
- L. angustifolia 'Rosea' – this cultivar has bright green leaves in

spring which fade to grey/green as the year progresses. The flowers appear from early summer and are pale pink to lavender in color. This plant grows to about 24"/60cm tall and 30"/70cm wide.

The following varieties produce white flowers:

- L. angustifolia 'Blue Mountain White' – pale grey/green leaves and pure white flowers from mid-summer onwards. Grows to 24"/60cm high and 32"/80cm wide.
- L. x intermedia 'Alba' – a vigorous plant with grey/green leaves and tall, white flowers blooming from late July. Grows up to 36"/90cm tall and between 36-48"/90-120cm wide.

The following cultivars are particularly good to grow if you are planning on drying the buds:

- L. x intermedia 'Provence' – has pale buds with a slight, camphor scent. The stem is easy to remove.
- L. x intermedia 'Grosso' – has a strong camphor scent from medium purple colored buds.
- L. angustifolia 'Royal Velvet' – dark purple buds that have a pleasant, sweet scent.
- L. angustifolia 'Buena Vista' – produces purple buds that have a very strong, traditional lavender scent.

The following varieties are grown for flowers to use in the kitchen:

- L. x intermedia 'Provence' – popular with meats and savory dishes.
- L. angustifolia 'Royal Velvet' – a dark purple bud that has a great flavor, making it particularly suited for desserts.
- L. angustifolia 'Betty's Blue' – a dark flower that has a pleasant

lavender flavor that is not overpowering.

- L. angustifolia 'Melissa' – a great flavor, popular in both teas and desserts.

These varieties are good to grow if you plan on crafting with lavender. These varieties are particularly good for wreaths because they produce flowers with long stems.

- L. angustifolia 'Folgate' – an early flowering variety that has dark blue/purple flowers when dried.
- L. angustifolia 'Royal Velvet' – dries dark purple.
- L. angustifolia 'Buena Vista' – dries dark purple.

The below cultivars are recommended if you are planning on producing essential oil:

- L. x intermedia 'Grosso' – this cultivar is considered to produce the largest amount of oil with a high camphor content.
- L. angustifolia 'Royal Velvet' – a good oil producing plant that has a sweet, more floral smell.
- L. x intermedia 'Super' – a lavandin producing a good quantity of oil with a pleasant fragrance.
- L. angustifolia 'Mailette' – popular in France where it is grown for its oil. Considered one of the best angustifolia varieties for oil.

HARVESTING, DRYING AND STORAGE

A popular, and easy, way to tidy up your lavender plants is to harvest the flowers. This gives you lots of dried flowers that you can use around your home for many different projects.

Lavandula angustifolia (English lavender) produces delicate flowers on long stems, protruding high above the plant. Lavandula stoechas (Spanish lavender) has shorter bracts of flowers. English lavender is considered better for crafting and culinary use in general as you have learned in the previous section.

English lavender is best harvested when the buds are fully formed, but the flowers have not quite opened. The flowers will also come off the stems much easier when they are dried plus they retain the color and smell for much longer. Of course, if you are doing this, then please plant a few extra lavender plants and allow them to flower so our friends the bees can have something to feed on!

The English lavender varieties Hidcote and Munstead are particularly good for drying, being recommended by a lot of people.

Lavender is very easy to harvest using a sharp pair of bypass secateurs/pruners or even scissors. Grab several long flower stems, leaving between two and four sets of leaves on the plant so that it can regrow easily from the cut. Remember that if you cut back to the wood stem, then that stem will not regrow. If you leave three or four sets of leaves when you harvest the flowers, it means you can prune the plant back a little further (to two sets of leaves) in the fall to keep it looking fantastic.

Continue harvesting flowers until you have a bundle that is between one and two inches across. Use twine to tie the bundle of flowers and then start cutting more fresh flowers to dry. Repeat this process until you either have enough flowers for your needs or have harvested the entire plant.

This method of pruning/harvesting keeps your plant healthy and encourages it to produce large amount of flowers every year. Careful pruning like this ensures your plants do not become leggy and that they look good in your garden.

Hang the lavender bunches somewhere warm and dry, out of direct sunlight, a shed, or garage is ideal for this. You can slowly dry it in your oven, but air drying tends to be the best way to dry lavender so it is in the best condition.

After two to four weeks, the lavender should be full dry. Gently rub or shake the buds onto a tray or into a large bowl.

Store fully dried buds in a sealed glass container in a cool, dark place until required.

LAVENDER IN THE KITCHEN

Lavender is undergoing a bit of a renaissance in the kitchen as chefs seek new and unusual flavors for their dishes. Used in the right quantities, it adds a delicate, floral note to food, but get the quantity wrong and the dish ends up tasting like your grandmother's perfume!

English lavender has the more pleasant smell and is more popular for cooking, with some recipes using the grey/green stems as a replacement for rosemary. The two most popular varieties for use in the kitchen are Munstead and Hidcote.

French lavender has more of a pine flavor than English lavender, so is less suitable for cooking. Spanish lavender is very similar to the French varieties and also has a flavor a little bit too strong for cooking.

When buying lavender for the kitchen, always buy culinary lavender, which means it has not been treated with harmful chemicals. If you grow your own, then avoid using any chemical sprays for a few weeks before harvesting or grow organically.

A little lavender goes a long way in a dish, so always start with a small quantity and add more slowly, tasting as you go to ensure that the dish does not take on a perfume like taste. Typically, you either grind the buds, which are then mixed with sugar, or steep them in a liquid, such as honey, and strain before use.

If a recipe calls for fresh lavender buds, you can use dried instead, though they tend to have a stronger flavor. For one part of fresh lavender buds, substitute with a third part of dried buds. So if a recipe calls for 3oz of fresh lavender buds, use just 1oz of dried in its place.

As a general rule of thumb, lavender pairs very well with bright, light flavors such as berries, mint, honey and lemon. It works very well in ice cream, cookies, breads and even some savory dishes where it is often used as a dry rub.

If you are cooking with fresh lavender, pick it as close to the time of use as possible. If you need to harvest it before hand, cut the flower stalks and place them in water until you are ready to use them. The shorter the time between harvesting and cooking, the more flavor and aroma is retained.

Lavender Recipes

There are lots of potential recipes you can make with lavender in them. Here are some of my favorite ones to give you some inspiration and ideas.

Lavender Sorbet

I love sorbet, and this recipe brings out the flavor of lavender. This dish makes for a great dessert as the lavender flavor is very refreshing after a meal. The recipe makes around 1½ pints of sorbet. Feel free to substitute the Concord grapes for another sweet red or purple variety that you can obtain locally, though be prepared to adjust the sugar content appropriately.

Ingredients:

- ½ cup white (granulated) sugar
- ½ cup water
- 1lb Concord grapes (stems removed)
- 2 tablespoons fresh lavender leaves

Method:

1. Boil the sugar and water in a small saucepan, stirring constantly
2. Remove from the heat, add the lavender leaves and cover
3. Leave for 10 minutes
4. Puree the grapes, then sieve into a bowl, discarding the solids
5. Add the lavender syrup, stir well, cover and refrigerate for 1-2 hours until cold
6. Chill a bread/loaf pan in your freezer for 10-20 minutes
7. Freeze, then churn the mixture in your ice cream maker (following the manufacturer's instructions)
8. Transfer to the pan, cover with plastic wrap and freeze for 2-3 hours until hardened

Lavender Cookies

Lavender works very well in baked goods and these cookies are no exception. This is a delicious, easy to make recipe that will produce 60-70 cookies. It takes around 30 minutes to make the recipe and then each batch of cookies is baked for 10 minutes. Note that you can replace the shortening with butter if you prefer. The shortening has a higher melting temperature than butter so helps to make for cookies with a uniform shape.

Ingredients:
- 2¼ cups all-purpose (plain) flour
- 1¼ cups white (granulated) sugar
- ½ cup butter (softened)
- ½ cup shortening
- 2 large eggs
- 4 teaspoons dried lavender flowers
- 1 teaspoon baking powder
- 1 teaspoon vanilla extract
- ½ teaspoon almond extract
- ½ teaspoon salt

Method:
1. Preheat your oven to 375F/190C
2. Cream the sugar, shortening and butter until light and fluffy (by hand or use a mixer)
3. Add the eggs, one at a time, beating well after each one
4. Add the vanilla and almond extract, then beat again
5. In a separate bowl, mix together the lavender, salt, baking powder and flour
6. Gradually beat this into the creamed butter
7. Drop rounded teaspoons of the cookie mixture on a greased baking sheet, spacing by 2"
8. Bake for 8-10 minutes until golden brown
9. Cool for 2 minutes, then transfer to wire racks
10. When completely cool, store in an airtight container

Lavender Chocolate Mousse

This is a very tasty chocolate mousse that is surprisingly easy to make. Add a tablespoon of Bourbon to give this mousse a bit of a kick!

Ingredients:

- 16oz heavy (double) cream
- 4 tablespoons cocoa
- 2 tablespoons confectioner's (icing) sugar
- 2 teaspoon dried lavender flowers
- 1 teaspoon vanilla extract
- 1 teaspoon instant coffee

Method:

1. Heat the cream slowly in a saucepan, stirring regularly, until it starts to steam
2. Add the lavender, remove from the heat and stir well
3. Steep for 20 minutes
4. Strain the lavender out of the cream, cover and refrigerate until cold
5. Add the rest of the ingredients to the cream
6. Whisk well, until thoroughly blended
7. Beat, using a mixer, until light and frothy
8. Spoon into cups, refrigerate and serve

Lavender Cupcakes
These cupcakes show off the flavor of lavender. Feel free to unleash your creativity in decorating these! This recipe makes 24 mini-cupcakes, though can be used to make full sized cupcakes but adjust the cooking time appropriately.

Ingredients:
- 1 cup all-purpose (plain) flour
- ½ cup white (granulated) sugar
- 2 large eggs
- 8 tablespoons (approximately 1 stick) butter (room temperature)
- 2 tablespoons milk
- 1½ teaspoons baking powder
- 1½ teaspoons dried lavender flowers
- 1 teaspoon lemon zest (grated)
- 1 teaspoon vanilla extract
- ½ teaspoon salt

Method:
1. Preheat your oven to 350F/190C and grease one or two muffin pans, depending on whether you are making large or small cupcakes
2. Process the lavender and sugar in your food processor for one minute
3. Put this sugar in the bowl of a stand mixer/food processor
4. Add the butter and beat until it is light and fluffy
5. Add the eggs, one at a time, beating after each one
6. Sift the flour, salt and baking powder into a bowl
7. Add the flour mixture to the butter mixture together with the milk, vanilla extract and lemon zest
8. Mix until just combined
9. Spoon into the muffin tin
10. Back for 12-15 minutes until a toothpick inserted into the middle of a cupcake comes out clean
11. Remove from the oven and cool before decorating

Lavender and Lemon Tea Cake

This is a tasty cake that combines the complimentary flavors of lavender and lemon. It is well worth making as the delicate lavender flavor will impress your afternoon tea guests!

Ingredients:
- 1½ cups all-purpose (plain) flour
- 1 cup white (granulated) sugar
- 1 cup plain yogurt
- ½ cup vegetable oil
- 3 extra-large eggs
- 2 teaspoons lemon zest (grated)
- 2 teaspoons baking powder
- ½ teaspoon vanilla extract
- ½ teaspoon salt

Glaze Ingredients:
- ⅓ cup lemon juice
- ⅓ cup white (granulated) sugar
- 2 teaspoons lavender buds

Method:
1. Preheat your oven to 350F/190C
2. Grease a 5½ x 9" loaf pan, lining the bottom with parchment (greaseproof) paper
3. Sift the salt, baking powder and flour together into a bowl
4. In a separate bowl, whisk together the eggs, yogurt, 1 cup of sugar, vanilla extract and lemon zest
5. Slowly add the dry ingredients to the wet, stirring as you do

6. Using a rubber spatula, fold the vegetable oil into this mixture, making sure it is well combined
7. Pour the mixture into the loaf pan
8. Bake for around 50 minutes until a cake tester pushed into the middle of the cake comes out clean
9. Cool in the pan for 10 minutes
10. Remove from the loaf pan and place on a sheet pan
11. Cook the glaze ingredients in a small pan, stirring often, until the sugar has dissolved
12. Put to one side for 20 minutes, then strain out the lavender buds
13. Pour the warm glaze over a warm cake and leave to soak in
14. Allow to cool fully before cutting

Lavender Dijon Dressing
This is a nice variation of the popular Dijon mustard that gives it a bit of extra flavor. It is great on any salad or in any situation where you would normally use Dijon mustard.

Ingredients:
- ½ cup extra-virgin olive oil
- 2 tablespoons Dijon mustard
- 2 tablespoons red wine vinegar
- 2 teaspoons dried lavender flowers (ground)
- ¾ teaspoon salt
- ½ teaspoon garlic (minced)
- ¼ teaspoon ground black pepper

Method:
1. Put all the ingredients in a jar, seal the lid and shake well to combine the ingredients
2. Alternatively, mix in a blender

Lavender Seasoned Meatballs

This recipe will make around 120 small meatballs with the delicate flavor of lavender. They are certainly unusual and the flavor combinations work very well together. Feel free to reduce the quantity to make fewer meatballs or just make larger meatballs, though remember to adjust the cooking time appropriately.

Ingredients:
- 2lb ground lamb
- 2lb ground beef mince
- 10 garlic cloves (minced)
- 2½ cups oatmeal
- 1½ fresh, chopped cilantro (coriander)
- ½ cup lemon juice
- ⅓ cup fresh thyme
- 2 tablespoons dried lavender (ground)
- 1 tablespoons salt
- 4 eggs
- 2 squirts of Worcestershire sauce

Method:
1. Mix all of the ingredients together in a large bowl, ensuring they are thoroughly combined
2. Use a melon baller to make meatballs of the same size, rolling between your hands to give them their shape
3. Brown the meatballs in a large frying pan with a little olive oil
4. Once browned, simmer for 5-8 minutes in their juices until cooked through

Herbes de Provence

This is the famous French herbs mixture used in French cuisine. It only takes a few minutes to make and this recipe will make about 11-12 tablespoons of the herb mixture. Store in a glass jar in a cool, dry place until required.

Ingredients:
- 3 tablespoons dried thyme
- 2 tablespoons dried parsley
- 2 tablespoons dried oregano
- 2 tablespoons dried savory
- 1 tablespoon dried lavender flowers
- 1 tablespoon dried marjoram
- 1 tablespoon dried rosemary

Method:
1. Mix all of the ingredients together in a bowl
2. Alternatively, blend in a spice grinder or grind with a mortar and pestle for a finer texture

Lavender Aioli

This Mediterranean sauce is a mixture of garlic and oil, popular in French, Italian and Spanish cuisine. It is similar to mayonnaise in texture. Thin the aioli with a couple of additional tablespoons of lemon juice to make a delicate sauce for vegetables. This recipe produces 6-8 servings.

Ingredients:
- 1 cup extra-virgin olive oil
- 6 garlic cloves (unpeeled and crushed)
- 3 eggs
- 2 sprigs of fresh lavender, including leaves and flowers (bruised)
- 1 tablespoon lemon juice

Method:
1. Add the oil, lavender and garlic to a small saucepan and heat gently
2. Simmer on a low heat for 15 minutes
3. Remove from the heat before the oil begins to bubble and leave to cool
4. When cool, strain the oil, pressing down on the mixture with the back of a spoon to extract soft solids from both the lavender and garlic

5. Discard the herbs
6. Process the lemon juice and eggs in your food processor until thoroughly combined
7. Add the oil with the blender still running in a thin, steady stream until it has all been absorbed and the mixture has thickened
8. Season to taste
9. Use immediately or refrigerate for up to two days (which will thicken it)

Lavender Salad

This is a great salad with a tangy dressing that brings out the lavender flavor. Feel free to use any salad vegetables you want in this recipe, which makes 8-10 servings.

Dressing Ingredients:
- 5 tablespoons extra-virgin olive oil
- 5 tablespoons lemon juice
- 1 teaspoon fresh ginger (grated)
- ½ teaspoon dried lavender flowers
- ½ teaspoon salt
- ¼ teaspoon Dijon mustard

Salad Ingredients:
- 8 cups mixed salad greens (washed and dried)
- 1 large red bell pepper (seeded and thinly sliced)
- 1 large peach/nectarine (sliced)
- 4 slices red onion
- 2oz feta cheese (crumbled)

Method:
1. Whisk the dressing ingredients together in a small bowl
2. In a large bowl, mix together all of the salad ingredients, except the feta cheese
3. When ready to serve, pour the dressing over the salad and toss well
4. Top with the feta cheese

Lavender Lemonade

This is a delicious drink that also helps relieve stress and headaches! It is very easy to make and a great product to have on your lemonade stand!

Ingredients:
- 12 cups of water
- 6 lemons
- 5 drops lavender oil (food grade)
- Honey (optional – to sweeten)

Method:
1. Squeeze the lemons into a drink pitcher
2. Add the rest of the ingredients and stir well
3. Chill before drinking

LAVENDER FOR BEAUTY

Like many herbs, lavender has a whole host of beauty uses. Both the essential oil and the fresh flowers and leaves can be used in your regular beauty regime. Before using lavender oil on your skin though, always patch test it first as some people can react to it. More on that in the Precautions and Safety section later.

Acne Buster

Acne tends to flare up when your skin does not have enough oil, so it overproduces sebum which then clogs your pores and causes acne. Lavender oil is good at moisturizing your skin, which reduces the sebum production plus it is antibacterial, so kills the bacteria that causes acne. Dilute lavender oil in a carrier oil such as coconut oil and apply it to your face using cotton wool after washing your face.

Mix two drops of lavender oil in a teaspoon of witch hazel to make an excellent facial toner. Soak a cotton ball in this and gently rub it over your face to tone your skin. If you have a problem spot, mix a drop of lavender oil with a drop of argan oil and apply directly to the pimple to reduce inflammation and speed healing.

Treats Dry Skin and Eczema

Dry skin and eczema are very unpleasant and the itching can drive you mad. Lavender oil balances the oil levels on your skin. Adding a few drops of lavender oil to a skin cream will help to alleviate the dry skin and keep your body properly moisturized. As lavender is both an anti-inflammatory and antifungal, it is very effective at reducing the effects of eczema.

Lavender oil is also good for treating psoriasis as it cleanses the skin, reduces the redness and alleviates irritation.

Mix two drops of lavender oil with two drops of tea tree oil and two teaspoons of coconut oil to make an excellent daily oil to apply to eczema or other skin conditions.

Skin Lightening
As lavender oil reduces inflammation, it can help to lighten skin, reducing dark spots and discoloration. It is also effective at lessening redness and blotchiness. Some people also use lavender oil to help with hyperpigmentation.

Facial Wrinkles
Fine lines and facial wrinkles are partly caused by free radicals. Lavender oil is packed full of antioxidants, which are well known to combat these harmful free radicals. Mix a few drops of lavender oil with some coconut oil and apply to your face as a moisturizer one or two times a day.

Anti-Inflammatory
Any skin inflammation can be treated with lavender oil to reduce pain and soothe the inflammation. Mix up to three drops of lavender oil with one or two teaspoons of coconut oil to make an effective, anti-inflammatory oil. Apply this to affected areas three times a day.

Lavender oil also helps to treat sunburn by making a spray that you apply to your skin. Mix together a quarter cup of aloe vera juice, 10-12 drops of lavender oil, 2 tablespoons of distilled water and jojoba oil as required. Pour into a spray bottle and shake well to ensure it is well mixed. Use two or three times a day until the sunburn has healed.

Wound Healing

Lavender oil helps to speed up wound healing, whether it is a cut, scrape or burn. According to a 2016 study, lavender oil promoted the healing of skin tissue (https://www.ncbi.nlm.nih.gov/pmc/articles/PMC4880962/).

Mix three or four drops of lavender oil with seven or eight drops of coconut oil. Apply the mixture, using a cotton ball, to your wound. If the wound has healed, continue to use this mixture to help reduce scarring.

Insect Repellent

Lavender oil is excellent as an insect repellent, but it is also good for treating itching from any bites. This oil is so effective at this, that it is a key component in a lot of the commercial mosquito repellents.

Candles and sprays work well as insect repellents. Add seven drops of lavender oil to a candle, then burn it outside when dry to repel insects. To make a spray, mix four drops of lavender oil in a spray bottle with eight ounces of water. Shake well, then spray on your body and clothes to repel insects!

Mix two drops of lavender oil with a carrier oil and apply to insect bites to prevent infection, reduce inflammation and ease pain. Adding a drop of peppermint oil to the mixture will help numb any pain. Apply this 2-4 times a day and it will relieve pain and prevent the bite from getting infected.

Lavender oil also works well to relieve irritation from the rashes caused by plants such as poison ivy.

Beauty Recipes

There are plenty of beauty products you can create from lavender. Here are some popular and useful recipes.

Hand Cream

This is an excellent hand cream that not only smells good, but is very effective at treating dry hands. It is ideal if you are a gardener or suffer from dry hands. As this is made using oils and beeswax, it is best applied when it has the time to soak into your hands, perhaps before going to bed at night. Until the oils have soaked in, avoid doing anything such as reading a book or using a computer where the oils could potentially damage what you are doing. This recipe will make about 6oz of hand cream. Use 2 tablespoons of beeswax for a thinner mixture that can work in a pump or 4 tablespoons for a stiffer mixture with a salve like consistency.

Ingredients:
- ⅓ cup sweet almond oil
- 1½oz/3 tablespoons grated beeswax
- 2 tablespoons extra-virgin olive oil
- 2 tablespoons coconut oil
- 30-35 drops lavender essential oil

Method:
1. Put all four oils in a small saucepan and stir together
2. Heat on a medium heat for about 5 minutes, until just about warm
3. Remove from the heat
4. Add the grated beeswax and stir until it has completely melted
5. Refrigerate for 5-10 minutes, until the oils begin to cool
6. Stir in the essential oil, using 35 drops if you want a stronger scent
7. Pour the cream into a container to cool
8. Store in a sealed container at room temperature for a softer cream and in your refrigerator for a stiffer cream

Lavender Soap
I love home-made soaps and think they are something really special. They are great to use yourself or to give as gifts and this lavender soap is no exception. This recipe will make three regular sized bars of soap. You will need soap molds for this as it is the easiest way to shape and harden the soap. Adjust the quantities of oil, flowers and colorant to your personal preference.

Ingredients:
- 1lb goats milk soap base
- Lavender oil
- Small handful lavender flowers
- Soap colorant (optional)

Method:
1. Cut the soap base into cubes
2. Melt in a double boiler over a low to medium heat
3. Add lavender oil and colorant to the soap base to your personal preference, stirring well
4. Add the lavender flowers and stir them in (note that they will float to the surface naturally which is okay)
5. Pour this mixture into your soap molds
6. Leave for at least an hour to harden
7. Remove the soap from the mold and wrap in greaseproof paper until required

Lavender Make-up Remover

This is a simple make-up remover that is really effective at getting your make-up off. When using, remove a cotton round, gently blot out excess liquid, close your eyes and wipe your face to remove your cosmetics. As an additional benefit, this moisturizes your skin and leaves it feeling wonderful. Add some tea tree oil to benefit from its antibacterial properties.

Ingredients:
- 2 tablespoons distilled water
- 2 tablespoons coconut oil
- 1 tablespoon witch hazel (non-alcoholic)
- 4 drops lavender essential oil
- Cotton rounds
- 4oz glass jar with a lid

Method:
1. Put 10 cotton rounds in your jar
2. In another jar, mix the coconut oil, water, lavender oil and witch hazel together, ensuring it is thoroughly combined
3. Pour this mixture into the jar containing the cotton rounds
4. Seal the lid and turn the jar upside down a few times to saturate the pads
5. Use as required

Lip Balm

This recipe makes about 5oz of lip balm, which will be plenty for you and your friends! It is really easy to make and will leave your lips feeling fantastic. Store this in small lip balm tins.

Ingredients:
- 3oz coconut oil (increase the amount of make a softer lip balm)
- 2oz beeswax (chopped or grated)
- 10 drop therapeutic grade lavender oil
- 5 drops vitamin E oil

Method:
1. Melt the beeswax and coconut oil together in a double boiler on a medium heat, stirring occasionally
2. Add the lavender oil and vitamin E
3. Remove from the heat and leave to cool for a couple of minutes
4. Pour (carefully) into the lip balm containers
5. Leave to cool until firm and enjoy

Lavender Bath Bombs

Bath bombs are cheap to make and great fun in the bath. Whether you are making them for yourself or as gifts, they smell divine and are good for your skin.

Ingredients:

- 1 cup baking soda
- ½ cup cornstarch
- ½ cup citric acid
- 3 tablespoons Epsom salts
- 2 teaspoons sweet almond oil
- ¾ teaspoon water
- 15 drop therapeutic grade lavender oil
- 3-5 tablespoons dried lavender flowers
- Bath bomb molds

Method:

1. In a large bowl, mix together the Epsom salts, cornstarch, baking soda, citric acid and dried lavender (use as much or as little of this as you want)
2. In a small bowl, mix the oils and water together
3. Pour the wet ingredients into the dry ingredients and whisk until fully combined
4. Press a handful of the mixture together to see if it holds
5. If it does not, lightly spray it with water once or twice and repeat until it is the right consistency
6. Press into the molds and leave for at least 2 hours to dry then remove
7. Leave on a soft towel overnight to dry fully

Lotion Bars

This is an easy recipe to make lotion bars that are great for your skin. These will be very helpful against dry skin, eczema or psoriasis.

Ingredients:
- ¼ cup Shea butter
- ¼ cup coconut oil (extra-virgin is best)
- ¼ cup beeswax
- ¼ teaspoon vitamin E oil
- 15-20 drops of lavender essential oil
- Soap colorant (optional)
- Silicone mold

Method:
1. Melt the Shea butter, beeswax and coconut oil carefully until they turn into a liquid (use a double boiler and grate/chop the beeswax)
2. Add the vitamin E oil and stir well
3. All to cool slightly
4. Add the lavender essential oil and stir well
5. Add any colorant that you are using, stirring well
6. Pour into the silicone molds and leave to cool

Whipped Body Butter

This is a great moisturizer for your skin and will help nourish it while alleviating inflammation and dry skin. Store in an airtight glass and apply after showering. If this feels a bit moist after whipping, leave it for a few hours and the consistency will improve.

Ingredients:
- 1 cup coconut oil (needs to be a solid at room temperature)
- 1 teaspoon vitamin E oil
- 10-15 drops lavender essential oil

Method:
1. Put all the ingredients into a mixing bowl
2. Using an electric whisk or stand mixer, whisk for 7-8 minutes, scraping down the sides regularly with a silicone spatula
3. Once it has taken on a light, airy consistency and has formed white peaks, it is ready
4. Transfer to an airtight glass jar, seal and use as required

Hair Conditioner

This is an excellent hair conditioner that is not only simply to make, but leaves your hair feeling soft and smooth. Instead of using lavender essential oil, try using rosemary, peppermint, clary sage or geranium, or any combination of the five oils, all of which are good for your hair.

Ingredients:
- 3 tablespoons coconut oil
- 1 tablespoon extra-virgin olive oil
- 8 drops lavender essential oil

Method:
1. Put all of the ingredients into a mixing bowl
2. Using a hand whisk, blender or stand mixer, whip the ingredients together on a medium to high speed for 5 minutes
3. Once a thick, creamy consistency has been achieved, apply to your hair
4. Comb through to evenly distribute, leave for 15-20 minutes and then rinse

Headache Treatment

The aroma of lavender is very calming and this mixture will help soothe any headache. Apply to your temples and forehead, being careful to avoid your eyes. The combination of oils and herbs will help to ease tension and relieve any pain.

Ingredients:
- 1oz beeswax (melted)
- 4 tablespoons extra-virgin olive oil
- 2 tablespoons Shea butter
- 1 tablespoon fresh lavender flowers or 1 teaspoon dried
- 1 tablespoon fresh lemon balm leaves or 1 teaspoon dried
- 1 tablespoon peppermint leaves or 1 teaspoon dried
- 50 drops peppermint essential oil
- 20 drops eucalyptus essential oil
- 15 drops rosemary essential oil
- 15 drops cajuput essential oil
- 5 drops lavender essential oil

Method:

1. If you are using fresh herbs rather than dried, pick them the day before, remove the flowers and leaves from the stems and leave overnight to wilt
2. Place the herbs in a muslin bag and tie the top
3. Put this bag into a glass and pour a cup of olive oil over it
4. Put a metal ring (such as those used on canning jars) in the bottom of a saucepan and place the glass on top of the ring
5. Full the saucepan with water until it is halfway up the side of the glass
6. Simmer on a medium heat for one hour, topping up the water as required, turning the bag and occasionally pressing the bag with the back of the spoon to encourage the herbs to infuse into the oil
7. Turn off the heat and put to one side
8. Once cool enough to handle, squeeze the bag to remove the infused oil from the herbs (use a potato ricer or similar for best results)
9. Put the infused oil back in the glass along with the beeswax and Shea butter
10. Place the glass on the metal ring, ensure the water level is high enough and simmer on a medium heat until both the beeswax and Shea butter have melted
11. Remove from the heat
12. Add the essential oils and stir until the mixture starts to thicken
13. Pour the salve into tins and allow to fully cool before sealing

LAVENDER – HEALTH AND HEALING

Lavender oil has a whole host of health benefits, with strong antiseptic and anti-inflammatory properties. It is useful for treating minor burns, dry skin, insect bites and more, but research indicates it has other uses for restlessness, depression, anxiety, insomnia and more.

Some studies indicate that lavender tea helps a number of digestive issues due to the inflammatory nature of the plant.

On top of this, studies show lavender to have antifungal properties too, https://www.ncbi.nlm.nih.gov/pmc/articles/PMC4621348/, and is particularly effective against fungal strains that affect your skin. Lavender essential oil has a property that destroys the membranes of fungal cells.

Lavender is commonly used to help heal minor wounds,

https://www.ncbi.nlm.nih.gov/pmc/articles/PMC4880962/, helping the skin to heal and repair itself. Studies have shown that lavender speeds the healing of wounds and research is underway into using this in a medical environment.

Lavender oil has also been noted to help prevent hair loss and improve hair growth, https://www.ncbi.nlm.nih.gov/pmc/articles/PMC4843973/. Mixing lavender oil into your shampoo or conditioner can help improve the quality of your hair and promote growth with several months of continued use.

The aroma of lavender is very relaxing and it appears to help reduce anxiety when visiting the dentist,. So if you suffer with anxiety when visiting the dentist, then inhaling lavender oil can help calm you down! See here, https://www.ncbi.nlm.nih.gov/pmc/articles/PMC4199191/, for more information.

This calming scent also helps alleviate premenstrual emotional symptoms, https://www.ncbi.nlm.nih.gov/pmc/articles/PMC3674979/. With this being a common problem for many women, no single treatment appears to be completely effective in reducing or eliminating these symptoms. The lavender oil alleviated these symptoms for the women involved in the study.

Be aware that at the time of writing, the United States Food and Drug Administration (FDA) has not approved lavender or lavender oil for medicinal use. It is sold purely as a supplement and should not replace any medicinal treatment prescribed by your doctor.

Precautions and Safety

Lavender, the herb, is generally safe to use, though obviously excessive quantities may cause some harm as with most herbs. The essential oil is generally safe for adults, though should not be digested. It can be used topically, but should always be diluted in a carrier oil or cream as it can cause a reaction in some people. You should always perform a patch test before using any lavender oil based product.

The biggest issue with lavender essential oil is that there are many different types of oil on the market. The fragrance oils are very cheap and should not be used topically, medicinally or in any beauty or culinary dish as the contents of the oil may be harmful. These are meant for burning or putting on pot pourri, not for using topically or internally.

The only oil you should use is therapeutic grade lavender essential oil, which is pure essential oil and nothing else. This is not cheap, but you know it does not contain any potentially harmful additives. This can be bought online or from most health shops and some supermarkets.

Lavender oil should not be used on young boys who have not been through puberty. This oil has a hormonal effect which disrupts their normal hormones and can, in some cases, cause gynecomastia or abnormal breast growth. The safety of lavender oil in young girls is not currently known.

Although some herbalists will recommend lavender oil to pregnant or breast feeding mothers, there is not enough research to determine the veracity of this. If you are pregnant or breast feeding, then it is best to avoid using lavender oil.

Lavender slows down the central nervous system as part of its relaxing properties. Therefore, if you are undergoing surgery, taking medications or having an anaesthetic, then stop using lavender at least two weeks before this. Only restart using lavender after consulting with your medical professional and confirming that it is okay to use this herb again.

Lavender also interacts with drugs that cause drowsiness and sleepiness. If you are on any drugs for these purposes, speak to your doctor before taking lavender. This herb is known to interact with chloral hydrate, increasing its effects and making you even more sleepy. It also interacts with sedatives such as barbiturates, including Amytal (amobarbital), Butisol (butabarbital), Luminal (phenobarbital), Mebaral (mephobarbital),

Nembutal (pentobarbital), and Seconal (secobarbital), amongst others.

Sedative medicines also have their effectiveness increased by lavender. If you are taking any sedative medication, including Ambien (zolphidem), Ativan (lorazepam), Donnatal (phenobarbital), and Klonopin (clonazepam), amongst others, you should not take lavender as it will cause you to become too sleepy.

Generally, lavender is safe to use, but if you are taking any medications you should consult with a qualified medical professional to ensure that it is safe for you to use lavender with your medications.

Health Recipes

There are a number of different ways you can use lavender to help you relax. Most of these use lavender essential oil, but in most cases, it is possible to substitute fresh lavender which will have similar results.

Relaxation
Add 5 drops of lavender essential oil to a bath together with some Epsom salts for a relaxing bath that will ease away the tensions of the day.

Better Sleep
Put a couple of drops of lavender essential oil on your pillow or in a diffuser at night. Alternatively, put a couple of sprigs of fresh lavender near your bed.

Air Freshener
Mix 10 drops of lavender essential oil with a teaspoon of witch hazel in a spray bottle and fill with water. Use this home-made air freshener on bedding, linen and in your closets to freshen items. Vary the scent by mixing in a few drops of lemon essential oil.

Body Butter
This is a simple body butter that you can make at home and use yourself or give as a gift. In warm weather, this may lose some of its whipped consistency, so just put it in the fridge and then whip it again to return it back to normal.

Ingredients:
- 1 cup coconut oil
- ½ cup Shea butter
- 10 drops lavender essential oil

Method:
1. Put all of the ingredients into your food processor
2. Pulse on a high setting for around 2 minutes until it has a whipped consistency
3. Remove and store in a glass jar

Baby Balm
This home-made balm is great for a baby's skin between diaper changes. The beeswax helps the balm to maintain its consistency.

Ingredients:
- 4 tablespoons coconut oil
- 1½ tablespoons beeswax pastilles (cosmetic grade)
- 10 drops lavender essential oil

Method:
1. Melt the coconut oil and beeswax in a double boiler
2. Once melted, remove from the heat and add the lavender oil
3. Pour into lip balm tins and leave for a few hours to cool

Bath Salts
These relaxing bath salts will relieve tension and stress while helping you sleep better. It can help alleviate minor aches and pains such as muscle or joint pain. Add 10 drops of peppermint oil if you are suffering from a cold as it will help relieve sinus pressure.

Ingredients:
- 2 cups Epsom salts
- ½ cup baking soda

- 25 drops lavender oil

Method:
1. Mix all of the ingredients in a bowl
2. Store in an airtight glass container until required
3. Use ¼ cup at a time in a bath

Antiseptic Spray
This is a pleasant antiseptic spray to use in your home or to use as a hand sanitizer.

Ingredients:
- 1 cup water
- 1 tablespoon witch hazel
- 2 teaspoons vitamin E oil
- 10 drops lavender essential oil
- 10 drops frankincense essential oil (optional)

Method:
1. Mix all the ingredients together
2. Transfer to a spray bottle
3. Use as required

Skin Repairer
This cream is used to help maintain a healthy skin as well as fight redness, moisturize and heal the skin. It is excellent for use after an acne breakout plus you can add additional oils to help heal bruising or scars.

Ingredients:
- 2oz coconut oil
- 1oz aloe vera juice
- 1oz Shea butter
- 1 teaspoon vitamin E oil
- 15 drops lavender oil

Method:
1. Mix the ingredients together in a mixing bowl
2. Blend with a hand mixer or food processor until light and fluffy
3. Store in a glass jar, applying to damp skin one to three times a day

Insect Repellent
Some people are naturally attractive to insects and get bitten dreadfully

during bug season. This home-made recipe is natural, good for your skin and contains no harmful chemicals. Store this in an 8oz spray bottle

Ingredients:
- 4oz water
- 3oz witch hazel
- 15 drops lavender oil
- 10 drops cinnamon oil
- 10 drops eucalyptus oil

Method:
1. Add all the ingredients to the spray bottle
2. Shake well to combine and then before each application

All About Lavender Oil

One of the most popular ways of using lavender is to use the essential oil. There are many different types of lavender oil on the market, and not all of them are essential oils. Many of the cheaper oils are perfume oils or otherwise watered down so they smell of lavender, but lack many of the healing properties of the plant. These cheaper oils also often additives to bulk them out, some of which are harmful if ingested or applied to the skin.

Always check that you are buying therapeutic or food grade essential oil as this is pure lavender and nothing else, so is considered safe. However, at the time of writing, lavender oil is not approved by the FDA, so there is no regulation or labelling requirements. Always buy your lavender oil from a reputable source so you know exactly what is in it. Generally, pure lavender oil is much more expensive than those that are diluted. In order to safely gain the benefits of lavender, you need a pure oil.

Lavender oil is one of the most popular essential oils, with people all over the world using it regularly. English lavender is considered to make the best oil, which is naturally the most expensive. However, the most common essential oil is made from lavandin, which is cheaper and considered inferior by many. However, as lavandin oil is cheaper, it is in high demand commercially, whereas home users tend to buy Lavandula angustifolia oil as less of it is required.

The difference between the oils is surprisingly easy to tell just by smelling them. Although the scent is similar, lavandin has a much stronger camphor smell, which reminds you of cold remedies. In lavandin, the camphor content is usually somewhere around the 6-8% mark whereas in true lavender, this is much lower, usually below 0.6%.

There are many different varieties of Lavandula angustifolia and the quality of the essential oil varies slightly between them all. Even the environment can influence the quality of the oil with variables such as type of soil, temperature, harvest time, plant age, amount of sun, water and food, all make a difference in the quality of the oil. Lavender farms will have a greater understanding of how these variables influence the quality of the oil and more resources to apply to oil manufacture. The home grower often has to make do with the environment and weather conditions that present themselves.

Some of the best lavender cultivars for producing oil are:

- Lavendula x intermedia 'Grosso' – the highest oil producing lavender, but it also has a high camphor content
- Lavandula angustifolia 'Royal Velvet' – a cultivar with a sweet, floral fragrance
- Lavendula x intermedia 'Super' – a lavandin cultivar that produces a lot of oil that smells very similar to Lavandula angustifolia
- Lavandule angustifolia 'Maillette' – one of the best angustifolia cultivars, popular in France where it is used to produce the essential oil.

It is possible to make your own lavender essential oil at home through steam distillation, but you need to be careful as in some areas it is illegal to distil anything as a still can be used to make alcohol! In order to produce a useable quantity of oil, you will need a lot of lavender.

Harvest the flower stalks and tie them together in bunches. Leave them to dry for several weeks, which prevents the oil from going rancid once it is produced plus it is easier to remove the flowers when they are dry.

When the flowers are completely dried, they can be steam distilled. This gives you a pure oil without any chemicals in, which you find with solvent extraction. The lavender is placed above boiling water, rather than sat in it, which prevents it from burning. The flowers are steamed, which extracts the oil that is then carried by the steam to a condenser where it cools and returns to the liquid state. The steam becomes a hydrosol, which can be used for skin care (see later on in this book for more), and the lavender oil is separated out. I would highly recommend visiting a lavender farm to see this process in action as it is fascinating to see it done on an industrial scale.

It is possible to do this yourself, but you do need a lot of lavender and for it to have dried completely before you start. If the lavender sprigs are not fully dry, then the lavender oil will be contaminated and becomes rancid.

This method makes a lavender oil but not necessarily a lavender essential oil.

Cut the flower from the plant with at least six inches of stalk. Try to cut them all to an even length. Use a rubber band to tie the lavender into bunches. Rubber bands are better than twine for this because as the lavender dries, it shrinks and when you use twine, the bunches will fall apart. Even with rubber bands, you will still find the odd stalk falling out of the bunch.

Hang the lavender cuttings upside down in a warm spot that gets some direct sunlight. It needs to be dry and have good air circulation. Leave the lavender for about two weeks, until completely dry.

Clean out a large glass jar and ensure it is completely dry. Fill it almost full with dried lavender, then cover with extra-virgin olive oil. Seal the jar and place on a window sill that gets some sun every day. Leave for up to six weeks to allow the sun to infuse the lavender into the oil. Strain the mixture and store the oil.

A quicker method involves using a crock pot. Fill the crock pot with 1 part dried lavender to 2 parts oil. Heat the crock pot on a low heat for 3-4 hours. Leave to cool, then strain.

Both these methods work well with olive oil, but also work with sunflower oil, jojoba oil, grapeseed oil and sweet almond oil. Any neutral, natural oil will work with these methods to produce a version of lavender oil you can use at home.

Popular Lavender Oil Blends

While lavender oil works wonderfully by itself, it can be mixed with other essential oils to enhance its properties and/or aroma. There are many different oils and blends, but the following are some of the more popular blends you can use. Mix these together and then apply them to your pillow or something you can sniff regularly such as a handkerchief, put in a burner, or mix with a little neutral cream and apply to your skin.

For relaxation:
- 5 drops lavender with 4 drops tangerine
- 2 drops each of lavender, lemon and peppermint

For better sleep:
- 4 drops lavender with 3 drops vetiver
- 4 drops lavender with 2 drops vetiver and one drop cedarwood
- 5 drops lavender with 2 drops frankincense
- 3 drops lavender with 3 drops cedarwood
- 2 drops each of lavender, vetiver and marjoram
- 2 drops each of lavender, marjoram and chamomile
- 3 drops each of lavender and bergamot
- 8 drops lavender with 2 drops clary sage

For improving your mood:
- 2 drops lavender with 4 drops tangerine, 1 drop each of lime and spearmint
- 2 drops each of lavender, lemon and rosemary
- 3 drops lavender with 3 drops bergamot and 2 drops clary sage
- 3 drops lavender with 4 drops orange and 2 drops frankincense
- 2 drops each of lavender and lemon with 1 drop each of rosemary

OTHER USES FOR LAVENDER

Lavender has plenty of different uses, as you have already found out. There are so many different things you can use lavender for, and this section is designed to introduce you to some of the other uses of lavender.

One of the popular uses for lavender is for crafts. There are plenty of things you can make from simple things like lavender wands to all sorts of other craft projects. Sites such as YouTube are full of examples of crafting with lavender, so is well worth looking at for some inspiration! One of the most popular things to make are little scented bags which you place in drawers to give your clothing a pleasant smell. These are made from dried lavender flowers and small bags, which can be store bought or hand-made.

Lavender vinegar is something worth making as this versatile vinegar can be used for everything from a hair rinse to a glass cleaner to a flea spray and even a fabric softener! It is really simple to make and worth having around your home.

All you need to make lavender vinegar is vinegar and lavender flowers. The most commonly used vinegar is distilled white vinegar, though you can use apple cider vinegar if you prefer. It is best to use fresh lavender flowers, though you can use dried if there are no fresh flowers available.

You need a glass jar that does not have a metallic lid. As you are working with vinegar, the lid can corrode during the infusing process and transfer an unpleasant, metallic taste to the lavender vinegar. A jar with a glass lid, such as a Kilner jar or similar is best to prevent contamination of the vinegar.

Fill a glass jar with lavender flowers, then cover with the vinegar. Seal immediately and store in a cool, dark place for 4-6 weeks. Every couple of days, give the jar a good shake. Once you have decided the infusing process is finished, strain the vinegar into a glass bottle and store in a dark place.

Lavender vinegar is a popular alternative to fabric condition that is particularly useful for anyone who suffers from allergies caused by fabric conditioned. Use a quarter of a cup of lavender vinegar in the fabric softener dispenser of your washing machine and top it up with water. Not only does this vinegar smell fantastic, but it is also naturally antibacterial. If you want a stronger lavender smell on your clothing, add a few drops of lavender essential oil to the fabric softener dispenser.

Lavender vinegar is also very repulsive to both fleas and ticks, so is excellent at keeping your home and pets free of this irritating pests without using harmful chemicals.

Mix equal parts of water and lavender vinegar in a spray bottle, shaking well before each use to ensure it is well combined. The effectiveness of this mixture can be enhanced by adding a few drops of insect repelling essential oils such as peppermint, eucalyptus and citronella.

Mist your dog and their bedding daily as well as before you take them outside and this will keep the fleas away from your dog. While this mixture is effective at repelling fleas, I do not recommend it for cats simply because cats hate being sprayed. From my experience, trying to spray a cat with anything usually involves a traumatized cat and a damaged human!

Another great use for lavender vinegar is as a window, glass or mirror cleaner. Vinegar has been used for a long time to clean glass and many of the commercial cleaners now contain some vinegar in an attempt to move away from harmful chemicals. However, you can easily make your own very cheaply that not only cleans well, but also leaves behind a pleasant smell.

Mix together 1 part water with 1 part vinegar and a tiny pinch of cornstarch. The latter ingredient is optional, but a tiny amount of cornstarch does seem to make the mixture clean better!

Apply the mixture to your windows using a cloth or crumpled newspapers, which was used years ago when vinegar was used as a cleaner.

Adding lavender vinegar to a bath helps to make it more relaxing as well as it being good for your skin. Combine this with some Epsom salts, and you have a very relaxing and healing bath.

Lavender vinegar has a whole host of uses, as you can see. It can also be used as a general purpose disinfectant, useful for cleaning toys, kitchen surfaces and more. While this does require a lot of lavender flowers to make, it is very useful to have around the home.

Lavender Bags

One popular use for dried lavender is to make lavender bags. These can be used yourself or given as gifts. They sit inside drawers and slowly release a lavender fragrance that makes the drawer smell nice and scents any clothing stored in the drawer.

Making lavender bags is very easy to do. You can either make your own bags, buy small drawstring bags or use decorative handkerchiefs instead. The nice thing about making your own bags, is you can choose a good quality material and then embroider the bags, which makes them excellent gifts!

Using a handkerchief is probably the easiest way to make a lavender bag. Spread your handkerchief out flat and then pile some dried lavender flowers in the middle of it. Carefully lift all four corners together and twist them slightly. Tie a ribbon or piece of string around this twist the keep the lavender flowers inside the handkerchief. For extra scent, try adding some dried rose petals to the lavender flowers. If you use a decorative handkerchief, then this can make a great gift too. These simple bags can be decorated by putting a fresh or dried sprig of lavender under the ribbon. Place the bag in your drawer and it will scent your clothing for several weeks.

Lavender Flower Water

Lavender flower water is the left over water from the steam distillation process that produces essential oil. It is also known as lavender hydrosol, hydroflorates or hydrolats. This water is a mixture of distilled water and lavender essential oil.

While many lavender farms bottle and sell flower water as a by-product, there are some distillers who specialize in producing this water. Experts consider the flower water from the early part of the distillation process to be superior to that from the middle or later parts.

The flower water contains all the same essences of lavender that the essential oil has, including the aroma, but it does not need diluting before use like an essential oil as it is not as concentrated.

Lavender flower water can be used in a similar manner to the essential oil. It is particularly good as a skin toner and can be applied directly. It can be used as a hair rinse as it will add a nice shine to your hair and leave it smelling pleasant.

Spray lavender flower water on your face to refresh and tone your skin. Apply it with cotton wool to help control breakouts.

Flower hydrosols are extremely beneficial to you and they contain hydrophilic (water loving) plant acids which make the water slightly acidic, which is good for your skin. This enhances the antiseptic and anti-inflammatory properties of the lavender as bacteria are not tolerant of acidic environments. Flower water is also a mild astringent, which helps to tone and firm skin while reducing blemishes and spots.

There are a multitude of uses for flower water from a body/face spray to treating acne and spots as well as to cool sunburnt skin. It can be used to mist a room to freshen the air, to spray linen and pillows for better sleep or in your iron to scent the clothes.

This by-product is surprisingly useful and can be used in many different ways. I like to mist some lavender water around my pillow at night so that it helps relax me and gets me to sleep. It is well worth trying!

One use for lavender flower water is to make a hair detangler. This helps make long hair more manageable, keeps it shiny, is good for the scalp and makes your hair smell great. It is particularly good for children's hair and helps you comb out tangles and knots.

Ingredients:
- 1 cup lavender flower water
- ½ teaspoon vitamin E oil
- ½ teaspoon jojoba oil
- 25-30 drops lavender essential oil

Method:
1. Mix the ingredients together in spray bottle
2. Shake well and use
3. Store in a cool, dark place when not in use

Growing your own zucchini is surprisingly easy to do. All you need is a packet of seeds of your chosen variety, some small pots (to start with) and some compost. In your local stores you will find two or three varieties of courgette at most, usually a green one, a yellow one and one other.

If you want to buy the more unusual varieties, then you will have to go online to the specialist seed providers where you will find as many as a couple of dozen varieties. I can recommend the more unusual, heritage varieties, rather than the F1 breeds as the heritage varieties usually have a much better taste.

ENDNOTE

Lavender is popular not only as a plant, but also as an ingredient in beauty, health or culinary recipes. It has been used by humans for centuries and is a popular scent that we are all familiar with.

It is very easy to grow lavender at home as it is a plant that is generally quite tolerant and tough plus it is bothered by few pests and problems. Whether you grow a couple of plants or create a lavender hedge, once the bees have finished with the flowers, there are plenty of things you can do with the fragrant remains.

So long as you get the soil right for lavender, i.e. ensure it is not too waterlogged, lavender will grow quite happily almost anywhere. It is happy in containers and in the ground and most varieties are at least frost hardy. Some of the more tender cultivars will need protection from the cold of winter, but they produce a beautiful display of instantly recognizable flowers.

Lavender is definitely an understated herb in the kitchen, probably because using too much of it, which is quite easy to do, gives dishes a perfume-like flavor. However, get the quantities right, and lavender can bring something very special to a dish. It is particularly well suited for desserts and sweet dishes, though is pleasant in some savory dishes.

The most common use of lavender is in the cosmetics industry, where it is used extensively for its distinct scent. Today, though, lavender is less popular than it was in the past and most people will remember their grandmother having at least something smelling of lavender. Saying that, lavender is still a popular scent and is very easy for you to use at home.

Like most herbs, lavender does have some healing properties. It is a useful antiseptic and is great for relaxation and helping you sleep. It has a whole host of other uses and is being extensively researched by scientists for its potential medicinal uses. It is already widely used by herbalists and self-prescribed by many people for its relaxing properties, but its use in medicine is potentially very exciting.

Lavender is grown commercially across the world and if you ever get the chance to visit a lavender farm, then I highly recommend it. Seeing fields and fields of lavender is spectacular plus the distillation process is fascinating to watch. Many lavender farms also keep bees and sell honey which has a hint of lavender to it, which is also delicious!

Growing lavender at home is very easy, providing you remember to ensure it has sufficient drainage and prune it regularly. Well kept, lavender will last for many years and makes a beautiful addition to any garden. It is a great plant to attract bees, butterflies and other pollinating insects and I love watching the wide variety of insects that pay a visit to my lavender plants.

You now know everything you need to know to grow lavender successfully at home. All you need to do is decide which variety, or even varieties, you want to grow! There are many different varieties with different color flowers, growing to different sizes and with different levels of hardiness. No matter where you live, there is a lavender variety that will grow for you.

Enjoy growing and using lavender, it really is a wonderful plant, and remember, please leave a review if you have enjoyed this book. I love hearing from my readers, so feel free to contact me through my website, http://www.gardeningwithjason.com or follow me on Instagram and Twitter as @Allotmentowner to keep up to date with what I am doing and share your garden pictures with me.

ABOUT JASON

Jason has been a keen gardener for over twenty years, having taken on numerous weed infested patches and turned them into productive vegetable gardens.

One of his first gardening experiences was digging over a 400 square foot garden in its entirety and turning it into a vegetable garden, much to the delight of his neighbors who all got free vegetables! It was through this experience that he discovered his love of gardening and started to learn more and more about the subject.

His first encounter with a greenhouse resulted in a tomato infested greenhouse but he soon learnt how to make the most of a greenhouse and now grows a wide variety of plants from grapes to squashes to tomatoes and more. Of course, his wife is delighted with his greenhouse as it means the windowsills in the house are no longer filled with seed trays every spring.

He is passionate about helping people learn to grow their own fresh produce and enjoy the many benefits that come with it, from the exercise of gardening to the nutrition of freshly picked produce. He often says that when you've tasted a freshly picked tomato you'll never want to buy another one from a store again!

Jason is also very active in the personal development community, having written books on self-help, including subjects such as motivation and confidence. He has also recorded over 80 hypnosis programs, being a fully qualified clinical hypnotist which he sells from his website www.MusicForChange.com.

He hopes that this book has been a pleasure for you to read and that you have learned a lot about the subject and welcomes your feedback either directly or through an Amazon review. This feedback is used to improve his books and provide better quality information for his readers.

Jason also loves to grow giant and unusual vegetables and is still planning on breaking the 400lb barrier with a giant pumpkin. He hopes that with his new allotment plot he'll be able to grow even more exciting vegetables to share with his readers.

OTHER BOOKS BY JASON

Please check out my other gardening books on Amazon, available in Kindle and paperback.

Berry Gardening – The Complete Guide to Berry Gardening from Gooseberries to Boysenberries and More
Who doesn't love fresh berries? Find out how you can grow many of the popular berries at home such as marionberries and blackberries and some of the more unusual like honeyberries and goji berries. A step by step guide to growing your own berries including pruning, propagating and more. Discover how you can grow a wide variety of berries at home in your garden or on your balcony.

Canning and Preserving at Home – A Complete Guide to Canning, Preserving and Storing Your Produce
A complete guide to storing your home-grown fruits and vegetables. Learn everything from how to freeze your produce to canning, making jams, jellies, and chutneys to dehydrating and more. Everything you need to know about storing your fresh produce, including some unusual methods of storage, some of which will encourage children to eat fresh fruit!

Companion Planting Secrets – Organic Gardening to Deter Pests and Increase Yield
Learn the secrets of natural and organic pest control with companion planting. This is a great way to increase your yield, produce better quality plants and work in harmony with nature. By attracting beneficial insects to your garden, you can naturally keep down harmful pests and reduce the damage they cause. You probably grow many of these companion plants already, but by repositioning them, you can reap the many benefits of this natural method of gardening.

Container Gardening - Growing Vegetables, Herbs & Flowers in Containers

A step by step guide showing you how to create your very own container garden. Whether you have no garden, little space or you want to grow specific plants, this book guides you through everything you need to know about planting a container garden from the different types of pots, to which plants thrive in containers to handy tips helping you avoid the common mistakes people make with containers.

Cooking with Zucchini - Delicious Recipes, Preserves and More With Courgettes: How To Deal With A Glut Of Zucchini And Love It!

Getting too many zucchinis from your plants? This book teaches you how to grow your own courgettes at home as well as showing you the many different varieties you could grow. Packed full of delicious recipes, you will learn everything from the famous zucchini chocolate cake to delicious main courses, snacks, and Paleo diet friendly raw recipes. The must have guide for anyone dealing with a glut of zucchini.

Environmentally Friendly Gardening – Your Guide to a Sustainable, Eco-Friendly Garden

With a looming environmental crisis, we are all looking to do our bit to save the environment. This book talks you through how to garden in harmony with nature and reduce your environmental impact. Learn how to eliminate the need for chemicals with clever techniques and eco-friendly alternatives. Discover today how you can become a more environmentally friendly gardener and still have a beautiful garden.

Greenhouse Gardening - A Beginners Guide to Growing Fruit and Vegetables All Year Round

A complete, step by step guide to owning your own greenhouse. Learn everything you need to know from sourcing greenhouses to building foundations to ensuring it survives high winds. This handy guide will teach you everything you need to know to grow a wide range of plants in your greenhouse, including tomatoes, chilies, squashes, zucchini and much more. Find out how you can benefit from a greenhouse today, they are more fun and less work than you might think!

Growing Brassicas – Growing Cruciferous Vegetables from Broccoli to Mooli to Wasabi and More

Brassicas are renowned for their health benefits and are packed full of vitamins. They are easy to grow at home but beset by problems. Find out how you can grow these amazing vegetables at home, including the incredibly beneficial plants broccoli and maca. Includes step by step growing guides plus delicious recipes for every recipe!

Growing Chilies – A Beginners Guide to Growing, Using & Surviving Chilies

Ever wanted to grow super-hot chilies? Or maybe you just want to grow your own chilies to add some flavor to your food? This book is your complete, step-by-step guide to growing chilies at home. With topics from selecting varieties to how to germinate seeds, you will learn everything you need to know to grow chilies successfully, even the notoriously difficult to grow varieties such as Carolina Reaper. With recipes for sauces, meals and making your own chili powder, you'll find everything you need to know to grow your own chili plants

Growing Fruit: The Complete Guide to Growing Fruit at Home

This is a complete guide to growing fruit from apricots to walnuts and everything in between. You will learn how to choose fruit plants, how to grow and care for them, how to store and preserve the fruit and much more. With recipes, advice, and tips this is the perfect book for anyone who wants to learn more about growing fruit at home, whether beginner or experienced gardener.

Growing Garlic – A Complete Guide to Growing, Harvesting & Using Garlic

Everything you need to know to grow this popular plant. Whether you are growing normal garlic or elephant garlic for cooking or health, you will find this book contains all the information you need. Traditionally a difficult crop to grow with a long growing season, you'll learn the exact conditions garlic needs, how to avoid the common problems people encounter and how to store your garlic for use all year round. A complete, step-by-step guide showing you precisely how to grow garlic at home.

Growing Herbs – A Beginners Guide to Growing, Using, Harvesting and Storing Herbs

A comprehensive guide to growing herbs at home, detailing 49 different herbs. Learn everything you need to know to grow these herbs from their preferred soil conditions to how to harvest and propagate them and more. Including recipes for health and beauty plus delicious dishes to make in your kitchen. This step-by-step guide is designed to teach you all about growing herbs at home, from a few herbs in containers to a fully-fledged herb garden. An indispensable guide to growing and using herbs.

Growing Giant Pumpkins – How to Grow Massive Pumpkins at Home

A complete step by step guide detailing everything you need to know to produce pumpkins weighing hundreds of pounds, if not edging into the thousands! Anyone can grow giant pumpkins at home, and this book gives you the insider secrets of the giant pumpkin growers showing you how to avoid the mistakes people commonly make when trying to grow a giant pumpkin. This is a complete guide detailing everything from preparing the soil to getting the right seeds to germinating the seeds and caring for your pumpkins.

Growing Tomatoes: Your Guide to Growing Delicious Tomatoes at Home

This is the definitive guide to growing delicious and fresh tomatoes at home. Teaching you everything from selecting seeds to planting and caring for your tomatoes as well as diagnosing problems this is the ideal book for anyone who wants to grow tomatoes at home. A comprehensive must have guide.

How to Compost – Turn Your Waste into Brown Gold

This is a complete step by step guide to making your own compost at home. Vital to any gardener, this book will explain everything from setting up your compost heap to how to ensure you get fresh compost in just a few weeks. A must have handbook for any gardener who wants their plants to benefit from home-made compost.

How to Grow Potatoes - The Guide to Choosing, Planting and Growing in Containers Or the Ground

Learn everything you need to know about growing potatoes at home. Discover the wide variety of potatoes you can grow, many delicious varieties you will never see in the shops. Find out the best way to grow potatoes at home, how to protect your plants from the many pests and diseases and how to store your harvest so you can enjoy fresh potatoes over winter. A complete step by step guide telling you everything you need to know to grow potatoes at home successfully.

Hydroponics: A Beginners Guide to Growing Food without Soil

Hydroponics is growing plants without soil, which is a fantastic idea for indoor gardens. It is surprisingly easy to set up, once you know what you are doing and is significantly more productive and quicker than growing in soil. This book will tell you everything you need to know to get started growing flowers, vegetables, and fruit hydroponically at home.

Indoor Gardening for Beginners: The Complete Guide to Growing Herbs, Flowers, Vegetables and Fruits in Your House
Discover how you can grow a wide variety of plants in your home. Whether you want to grow herbs for cooking, vegetables or a decorative plant display, this book tells you everything you need to know. Learn which plants to keep in your home to purify the air and remove harmful chemicals and how to successfully grow plants from cacti to flowers to carnivorous plants.

Keeping Chickens for Beginners – Keeping Backyard Chickens from Coops to Feeding to Care and More
Chickens are becoming very popular to keep at home, but it isn't something you should leap into without the right information. This book guides you through everything you need to know to keep chickens from decided what breed to what coop to how to feed them, look after them and keep your chickens healthy and producing eggs. This is your complete guide to owning chickens, with absolutely everything you need to know to get started and successfully keep chickens at home.

Raised Bed Gardening – A Guide to Growing Vegetables In Raised Beds
Learn why raised beds are such an efficient and effortless way to garden as you discover the benefits of no-dig gardening, denser planting and less bending, ideal for anyone who hates weeding or suffers from back pain. You will learn everything you need to know to build your own raised beds, plant them and ensure they are highly productive.

Save Our Bees – Your Guide to Creating a Bee Friendly Environment
Discover the plight of our bees and why they desperately need all of our help. Find out all about the different bees, how they are harmless, yet a vital part of our food chain. This book teaches you all about bees and how you can create a bee friendly environment in your neighborhood. You will learn the plants bees love, where they need to live and what plants are dangerous for bees, plus lots, lots more.

Vertical Gardening: Maximum Productivity, Minimum Space
This is an exciting form of gardening allows you to grow large amounts of fruit and vegetables in small areas, maximizing your use of space. Whether you have a large garden, an allotment or just a small balcony, you will be able to grow more delicious fresh produce. Find out how I grew over 70 strawberry plants in just three feet of ground space and more in this detailed guide.

Worm Farming: Creating Compost at Home with Vermiculture
Learn about this amazing way of producing high-quality compost at home
by recycling your kitchen waste. Worms break it down and produce a
sought after, highly nutritious compost that your plants will thrive in. No
matter how big your garden you will be able to create your own worm farm
and compost using the techniques in this step-by-step guide. Learn how to
start worm farming and producing your own high-quality compost at
home.

WANT MORE INSPIRING GARDENING IDEAS?

This book is part of the Inspiring Gardening Ideas series. Bringing you the best books anywhere on how to get the most from your garden or allotment. Please remember to leave a review on Amazon once you have finished this book as it helps me continually improve my books.

You can find out about more wonderful books just like this one at: www.GardeningWithJason.com

Follow me at www.YouTube.com/OwningAnAllotment for my video diary and tips. Join me on Facebook for regular updates and discussions at www.Facebook.com/OwningAnAllotment.

Find me on Instagram and Twitter as @allotmentowner where I post regular updates, offers and gardening news. Follow me today and let's catch up in person!

FREE BOOK!

Visit http://gardeningwithjason.com/your-free-book/ now for your free copy of my book "Environmentally Friendly Gardening" sent to your inbox. Discover today how you can become a more eco-friendly gardener and help us all make the world a better place.

This book is full of tips and advice, helping you to reduce your need for chemicals and work in harmony with nature to improve the environment. With the looming crisis, there is something we can all do in our gardens, no matter how big or small they are and they can still look fantastic!

Thank you for reading!